CONTENT

DEDICATION

I gleefully dedicate this book to my ENTIRE family! My son, Antonio, who willingly assisted and helped me by sharing his creativity with this book. And my Love who patiently stood by me and encouraged me.

ABOUT THE AUTHOR

I am a woman from a small town who experienced growing up as a minority. I had two parents that worked, a brother and sister that sometimes played with me, teamed up against me, and ignored me (normal). Oh, and they told lies on me too. I was a perfect angel. Okay, so that's not completely true. I truly love my family and that's all that matters! We were considered a middle class family. I grew up with cats and dogs, rode my bike in our safe neighborhood, and I loved shopping with my mom (still do). During my school years, I had good teachers and friends. Everything sounds lovely doesn't it? Of course my life was not perfect. Did I mention that my family was one of the first black family's in my neighborhood and at our schools in the beginning? Our lives were very...interesting.

What I remember most about my first experiences regarding lies and omissions was mostly during middle school (junior high) thanks to a particular person I thought at the time was my friend. I'll tell you more about that later in this book. As I grew older, life taught me many lessons as I'm sure it has taught all of you out there. You could probably write your own book! Anyway, I did not sail through life to the point where I am now, without being unscathed. I went through my academics and completed two Bachelor degrees and a Master's degree. I'm a proud mom (including my fur babies), daughter, sister, best friend, girlfriend and friend.

INTRODUCTION

WELCOME! Thank you so much for taking the time to read my book. Have you ever wanted to write a book and thought to yourself, "Self, what do we all have in common?" That is how I came up with this book. We all know other people who have told lies and who simply just keep information to themselves. Let's keep it real, we, ourselves, have lied and omitted information too but to what degree? I'm not saying you are a bad person if you tell lies or omit information. I'm saying it's the receiver of your lies and/or omissions that it will affect. So the only person or people who can have an opinion that matters one way or the other about it are the individuals involved. Not me.

I hope this book broadens your perspective, makes you think before you take any action and be empathetic or sympathetic. Above all, stand up for yourself and those you care about! Just be a better version of yourself. We all have choices to make. When we come to that fork in the road (to lie, omit or tell the truth) which one will you choose? How will it affect the other person or yourself? What if you were the receiver of the lie or omission? Trust and believe, one size does not fit all.

WHAT IS IMPORTANT TO YOU?

Your reputation, social standing, how you are perceived, material items, or the fact you want to be right perhaps...

WHO IS LYING OR WITHHOLDING?

For some individuals, lying comes very easily but knowing when to stop is most important. Can you imagine being around a habitual liar? Personally, it has driven me nuts and I could not wait to remove myself from those individuals, but that's just me. My own sanity is of utmost importance, especially now. Others who may have more tolerance, may stick around and accept the person and/or try to help in some way. However, as far as I know, there is no cure for a habitual liar.

Or what about omission? I would think to myself (if I found out about the omission), why? Or I can't believe it! Or that stinking mother f-er! Or ok, no biggie. It all depends, doesn't it? On the flip side, what if you (or I) is the person withholding? You may want to ask yourself about the person you are omitting information from. Is the omission for your own good or theirs? What happens if the omission were to be revealed by someone else! Before you had a chance to tell your truth. What would the ramifications be for goodness sake? How important is the omission to you? Could you go on with your daily life talking and acting normal knowing you should not omit information? If you can say to yourself, I will take this to my grave and have no problem with it, then fine-cool. Or, if it bothers you in the slightest, have the courage to set yourself free, and let that individual know what is on your mind. Right the wrong.

Does it matter if someone is lying or has lied to you? Or worse, lied about you! What about just omitting information? Hell yeah it matters! What if the individual was a close family member, a best friend, lover, wife, husband, confidant, co-worker, boss...I could go on and on. It could change the whole dynamic of your relationship with not only the individual, but others that you both may know! It could be a domino effect.

For example, you are in your workplace and overhear two people talking about taking the majority of the credit for a group project you and two others are in. The project just made the company several hundred thousand dollars. The president wants to congratulate the group by taking the group out to dinner, providing bonuses in your next checks, and making an announcement in next month's company newsletter. You know everyone in the group and how much or little each contributed. You were just one of the individuals who worked your butt off! Generally speaking, you don't like or dislike these two who plan to lie. Until now. Do you confront the two soon to be liars? Do you tell the others in the group? Do you tell the President of the company? If so, before or after the congratulatory dinner, check bonus, and newsletter? Or, do you omit the information and do nothing, maybe wait for another opportunity if it arrives?

Would telling or not telling affect your job? What a conundrum! I personally would not tell nor omit. You might ask me, how can you not do both? Well, you should be able to think about what is best for yourself and the others that worked just as hard as you did. Not to mention the timing of the situation. During the celebratory dinner while everyone is talking about the project, you could simply ask a few questions about what one (or both) did to accomplish the tasks they didn't actually do. Letting that go would be a no, no. It's likely the two would take another opportunity to lie again.

DOES SIZE MATTER?

Get your mind out of the gutter! Of course size matters. The size of the lie or omission could prove to be disastrous or not even make a crack in your foundation. By now you could surmise that who does the lying and/or omission matters, depending on their relationship with you or your relationship with them. You'll see what I mean.

You have two best friends, Richard and Patrick, both you've known for quite some time. Richard and Patrick know of each other but only through you, otherwise, not really. On one occasion, you and Richard are hanging out and Richard meets a young lady by the name of Ava. Richard and Ava hit it off and you see some flirting taking place. Ava is coming on pretty strong to Richard. So far, you are just observing. The day was long and fun. Evening arrives, Richard pulls you aside and confides his feelings for Ava and is considering taking her to his place.

Patrick, you and other cool friends hang out whenever you get the chance. You live far from Patrick so you don't get to spend as much time with him and everyone else as much as you'd like. Patrick has an "unofficial" girlfriend. She is a part of the group of friends that hang out together. However, everyone in the group knows that Patrick is considering asking his "unofficial" girlfriend Ava to be his officially.

Yes, that is right! Ava likes both of your best friends. She and Patrick have been friends for a long time. They know each other by attending the same schools years ago. Richard and Ava just met, yet when Richard falls for a young lady, he falls hard. You find yourself caught in the middle. Both guys are your best friends. You do not want to see either one hurt. What should you do? If you say something, you might destroy one of your friendships.

Before I tell you what actually happened, this is a true story with some minor changes. I am a strong believer in friendships. True friends are not easy to come by. Associates, on the other hand, come and go. Hold on to your true friends. Friends are the individuals that accept you for who you are and all the baggage you come with and vice versa.

Usually, you go to your best friends for advice but in this situation, who do you talk to? I'd advise talking to someone that doesn't know your friends. Someone who will provide unbiased advice. Such as a therapist if you know one and are open to it. If you are not open to speaking to a therapist directly, you could always read books on relationships by professional therapists or others.

In the end, this is what happened. You tell Richard that you actually know Ava and how you know Ava (through your other group of friends). You let him know that Ava is very close to your other best friend Patrick. You make it clear that they are more than just friends but not official, yet. You also talk to Patrick and let him know that Ava met your other best friend (include dates) and that she likes him for more than a friend as well. Explain as best you can to both of them that you only have their best interest at heart and you felt they should know the situation. That's it! What each person, Richard and Patrick does after that is totally up to them and Ava. What about Ava you ask? She is not your best friend and she knows you are best friends with the two men she likes. Now, you stay out of it.

If you're into books like I am, I recommend the book by Gurman, A.S., Lebow, J. L. & Snyder, D.K. (2023). *Clinical Handbook of Couple Therapy (6th ed.).* New York: Guilford. In my opinion, you don't actually have to be a "couple" to reap the benefits of this book.

THE SITUATION

Let me begin by saying, it does not matter where you come from, your ethnic background, your social standing, whether you are male or female, heterosexual, LGBTQIA +, you're young, or old anyone can lie and/or omit information. The outcome is hurt, pain, dismay, and disbelief, etc. I have a soft spot in my heart for anyone who has experienced racism or bigotry. Especially if you have experienced it as a teenager and in school. There are those who still have scars today from what they've been through. The experience can change your whole life. We do not forget. For those of you out there that have inflicted the words and acts. We do not forget. Some might thank you for influencing the person we are today. Others, not so much.

What do I mean by the situation? I mean what are the circumstances? The two situations I spoke about previously were pretty serious. Well, what if it's not so serious, then what? It all comes down to where you stand and who is involved. A matter of morals let's say. You can always be selective about your involvement and make your decisions based on past experience. Making a decision to stay out of people's business and/or personal lives can be the best decision sometimes. No matter who is involved. However, sometimes, you may try your best to stay out of a situation but find yourself a part of the situation because you are the target.

Remember when I introduced myself in the beginning of this book? I spoke about a particular someone I thought was my friend in middle school. Here is my situation. I will not be using real names in this story but you know who you are. I was in elementary school when I met Cami. It was another black family moving into my neighborhood. I was excited! I think I was in 4th or 5th grade when we met. I thought we hit it off as friends. We would ride our bikes to each other's houses and hang out. We'd ride to the store to buy candy. I loved the green apple jolly rancher sticks. Riding our bikes was the main part of transportation and independence back then. Things started to change between Cami and myself, and as individuals when we started middle school. As we all know, that's when hormones kick in (for most of us). My hormones kicked in the latter part of elementary school. Social status becomes more important, who you talk to and make friends with is important, extra curricular activities in and out of school becomes more of a big deal. Practically everything is important at that time, boys ...uugh.

I had met a boy in school that was Hawaiian, his name was Kai. I thought Kai was very cute. I shared with Cami that I liked him and thought he was cute. I don't remember the exact time frame but not long afterwards he told me in the hallway that he knew I thought he was cute. If I could have disintegrated at that moment, I would have! He told me that Cami told him what I said. I didn't realize at the time that she was being deceitful but it all worked out in my favor. Another moment with Cami was when we were in the girls bathroom looking in the mirror primping, she mentioned something like, "I hate it when people have big spaces under their eyebrows". Of course the first thing I did was look at my eyes. Apparently, I didn't see what she saw so it didn't bother me at that time. A significant moment arose when we rode our bike out one day. Cami was very happy and told me her best friend and her big sister were moving to our town. She told me she couldn't wait for me to meet them. She told them all about me. I was happy at that time and was looking forward to it.

True to her word, Cami's best girlfriend Olga and her big sister Helga moved in and attended our school. It didn't take long at all for Cami to drop kick me to the curb and have Olga and Helga start being mean to me. Till this day, I don't know why (and could care less). Most of the time, I walked to school, especially during the winter season, instead of riding my bike. I remember walking home; Cami, Olga and Helga would walk very close behind me and insult me in every way they could think of. In school, Olga and Helga would yell down the hallway and call me a nigger.

Yeah, that pissed me off! What was totally messed up for me? Cami was as black as I was and she was their best friend! All three would spread lies about me. I had other friends of mine confide in me about what was being said. This went on for a long, long time, the taunting got so bad. I involved my mother and older sister. My mom and sister stuck up for me but also strongly suggested I stick up for myself. I finally did. I would say things back, argue with them, exchange mean and dirty looks, etc. One day Olga told me her older sister Helga wanted to fight me after school. I do not remember what I said but it was arranged. We had tennis courts at our school. There was a walkway leading from the school down to the tennis courts and up to the sidewalk that led home. When you walked past the tennis courts you'd see rocks in between the walkway and the fence of the court. I'm pretty sure other kids were around. That was where the bike riders and walkers had to pass by to get home. All I can tell you is that I was sick of the three of them and wanted to get those B's out of my life.

I honestly cannot not remember if Cami was there or not. She wasn't on my mind at the time. It was Olga, Helga and myself. We were by the tennis courts yelling and arguing. Helga made the first move. I pushed Helga and she landed up against the court fence and slid down on top of the rocks. She then started to laugh. I told her to get her ass up, Olga told her to get up too but she wouldn't, she just kept laughing. I looked at Olga and said something, got on my bike and rode home.

Middle school lasted for an extremely long 3 years (6th, 7th and 8th grades). We were the first class in my town to start the 6th grade in junior high. The schools changed it and the name became middle school. It has been like that ever since. I went to a different high school than Cami, Olga and Helga because of the way the school district was divided. I actually think Olga and Helga moved again. Don't think that just because I went to a different high school the lies and roomers stopped, oh no! One day, a boy I knew was walking past my house and we waved hello. He came up into my driveway asked how I was doing and blah blah blah. Then he told me I didn't look pregnant. I laughed and asked what?! He told me that someone had told him I was pregnant. I assured him I was not. I told him to tell Cami and anyone else who cared that I was not. He just laughed and wondered how I knew who said it.

I had no idea I was still on her mind at the time. She sure as hell wasn't on mine.

As an adult, I realized I was bullied in school. During that time, people were not focused on it as much as they are today. The way schools handle bullying now has changed so much since then. The way kids behave has changed so much since then. It seems like they are more selfish these days and don't care about consequences. For those parents that have kids being bullied during this time of computers, cell phones and all of the different social media platforms, I feel for all of you and your children.

THE SIGNS

Do you know how to tell if someone is lying to you? Everyone lies, some more than others. The average person lies approximately 4 to 5 times a day. Is that a lot? I really don't know. I would just be concerned about the degree and from whom the lie is coming. If you know someone well enough, I believe it would be easier to tell if they are lying as opposed to someone you do not know very well. Since neither you nor I have a magic wand, we'll have to rely on our instincts and other signs.

VERBAL, BODY LANGUAGE, AND EVIDENCE

"No single technique should be used alone as a determining factor for catching someone in a lie for personal or law enforcement purposes. Researchers do their best to design studies that isolate specific evidence, but every situation is unique and should be handled carefully depending on the circumstances." as stated by <u>Rachel Drummond, MEd.</u>

Here are some popular signs to tell if the person you know is lying:

- The person changes the way they normally talk (they talk faster, or slower and more carefully, their voice pitch usually goes up an octave or more.

- What the person says and does is the opposite of each other. If the individual points right but looks left, you should probably go left.

- If you ask someone you know a simple question and their answer is long and drawn out or extremely short. That is a red flag.

- It's all in the eyes. Does the person you know normally look away or around when they speak to you or look directly at your face while talking? If they do the opposite of what they normally do, more than likely they're lying.

- If you have a child or children, you'll know this one. The inability to keep still when you ask a question and you both know a lie is forming in their head. I believe some people carry that behavior into adulthood.

- Physical evidence is always a plus in having proof that someone told a lie. Be patient, it might not be found when you want it or need it.

NOW WHAT?

It's all out in the open; You know, I know, they know, we all know...so?

REVELATIONS!

However you figure out the truth or whatever has been omitted comes to light, depending on how big it is, an individual might be a bit emotional. Those emotions could set off positive or negative actions or reactions. If you know the individual, it may be easy to predict what you think would happen in a given situation after a person finds out the truth but in reality, neither party will ever know until it is revealed. So be careful.

Did you know that there is a difference between how men react to finding out they've been lied to and cheated on vs how women react to finding out they've been lied to and cheated on? I did. Men tend to separate themselves from the act of lying and cheating. They have the ability to compartmentalize their situations. When he is with woman A, he doesn't think about woman B (and vice versa). It's not until someone finds out he's being dishonest that woman A and B are combined. It is just how their minds work. They have the ability to compartmentalize in pretty much all situations in their lives, such as business, hanging out with their friends, sports, women, and family.

This is what women can not seem to grasp about men and their ability to "step out". Men can't seem to figure out why women get so upset and may want to leave them for the act. For men, "infidelity can be an opportunistic, primarily sexual action that, in their minds, does not affect their primary relationship. In fact, when asked, many such men will report that they're very happy in their primary relationship, that they love their significant other, that their sex life is great, and that, despite their cheating, they have no intention of ending their primary relationship." as stated by Robert Weiss Ph.D., LCSW, CSAT.

Women's minds are definitely different when it comes to lying, cheating and omission of information. According to Robert Weiss, Ph.D., LCSW, CSAT, "Women are less likely to operate the same way. For most women, a sense of relational intimacy is every bit as important as the sex; often more important. As such, women tend to not cheat unless they feel either unhappiness in their primary relationship or an intimate connection with their extracurricular partner — and either could cause a woman to move on from her primary relationship."

If a woman finds out that her boyfriend, man,

or husband has lied about having an outside relationship or omitted being in a relationship already. Her response is going to be an emotional one for sure. It is her emotions that will more than likely keep her in the relationship regardless of being cheated on and lied to, generally speaking. Women consider love, intimacy, longevity and her future with her partner when making life altering decisions. That is what women consider in choosing their mate in the beginning when they are single. This is precisely why women who are not happy in their current relationships lie, cheat and omit information from men.

On the flip side, generally speaking, if a man comes to the realization that his girlfriend, woman, or wife has cheated on him he will tend to behave irrationally in the beginning because he is thinking of the physical act of her cheating not the emotional act. React now and think later. A man knows if a woman decides to "step out", she is emotionally invested in the other person and there could be a possibility that she could leave because she is unhappy. Men realize that they are no longer the woman's main focus and it scares them. Men tend to feel more betrayed because of a woman's emotional connections to another person. The relationship is less likely to survive because of the man's inability to rationalize that there is still a possibility to salvage the relationship. For those men who are more rational, they may have a better chance to reconcile.

ONLY HUMAN

*"**An Essay on Criticism** is one of the first major poems written by the English writer Alexander Pope (1688–1744), published in 1711. It is the source of the famous quotations* **"To err is human; to forgive, divine"**, **"A little learning is a dang'rous thing"** (frequently misquoted as "A little knowledge is a dang'rous thing"), and **"Fools rush in where angels fear to tread"**, *as stated in Wikipedia,The Free Encyclopedia.*

Are you a product of your environment? Some would argue YES! While others would argue NO, that's just an excuse! I have witnessed people adapting to their environment regardless of where they are originally from or how they grew up. Can you take a docile child from a close knit family oriented town and move that child to a big city where they have to learn to fend for themselves and expect that child to stay the same? The average person has the ability to learn and grow as they age. You can learn from your mistakes. You will make new mistakes. You have a choice of whom you hang around as an adult. You have the choice to lie or omit. Others have the choice to stay, flee, forgive, or not forgive.

RECONCILE OR KEEP IT MOVING?

Are you a religious individual? Spiritual? Believe in the Divine Being(s)? Is your advice to others to "turn the other cheek?" How about yourself? I could imagine that to reconcile or not, would be a difficult decision for anyone. Looking from the outside, so to speak, it may seem easy. People pass out advice (welcomed or not) like it's an infinite amount of candy! There are so many variables to take into consideration; Who did it involve? What happened? Where did it happen, When? and Why?

People are vulnerable. We, you and I may forgive but do we forget? I've heard it often, "You have to learn how to forgive". It is not impossible to forgive and reconcile, it happens all the time. Individuals are just prone to hear, see, or be surrounded by more of the negative than the positive. I think if we witnessed more of the positive, we would be more prone to forgive.

Regardless of the outcome of being the receiver of lies or omissions, or being the liar and/or the one who omits, I hope you don't stay stuck and keep it moving! Whatever that means for you, take the experience and share it with others and put it out there. You will figure out that you are not alone. Having the ability to share experiences can be healing and cathartic. Earlier I suggested therapy or seeking the help of other professions, check it out. There is no shame in creating personal growth for yourself and/or others that you may affect. Don't knock it, until you try it!

CONCLUSION

We all lie and omit. If you say to anyone or to yourself that you have never lied or omitted anything, you are doing it RIGHT NOW. Have you figured it out? Which is worse, the lie or omission? The answer is (drum roll) you need to re-read this book to figure it out. Who and what is important to you?

You could be anonymous, I suppose, in given situations if you didn't want to be known to be the one to shake things up and reveal the truth. If you are the liar or omit information, it's your choice to continue to stay on the path you're on. Do not use excuses if that is your decision. You may be correct in your thinking (or not). I would like you to just consider what was written in this book. The size of the lie and omission does matter.

You know the world is not going to end if your adult daughter tells you she's out with her girlfriend but omits that her girlfriend is actually her lover. Why might she omit that information? Consider who the lie or omission affects more in the long run. Is the entire situation affecting a lot of people, a small group or just a couple of people. It is easier to come through a lie or omission if less people are involved. The possibility of getting caught or found out by your own actions is the hardest because there is no one else to blame.

Regarding the thought of forgiveness, it is easier to stay mad and really hard to forgive but consider your health and those you care about. Stress can kill you. Reconciliation in any relationship is possible if you can get past yourself. Realize that there is relief in having the courage to tell your truth and knowing you are not alone. Help is out there if you so desire. Keep it moving!

RESOURCES

RESOURCES

1. Merriam-Webster. (n.d.). Dictionary by Merriam-Webster. In *Merriam-Webster*.

https://www.merriam-webster.com/

1. MEd, B. R. D. (2024, February 1). *10 Top Signs That Someone is Lying - How to Know*. Forensics Colleges.

https://www.forensicscolleges.com/blog/resources/10-signs-someone-is-lying

1. Wikipedia contributors. (2024, July 11). *An essay on criticism*. Wikipedia. https://en.wikipedia.org/wiki/An_Essay_on_Criticism
2. Robert Weiss Ph.D., LCSW, CSAT (2017, July 10). Why Men and Women React to Infidelity So Differently... and why one has a more developed inner detective.

https://www.psychologytoday.com/us/blog/love-and-sex-in-the-digital-age/201707/why-men-and-women-react-to-infidelity-so-differently

9 798338 342909